All About Neymar Jr.

Inspiring stories, facts, and trivia about a soccer superstar

All the history, details and incredible feats you need to know as a superfan of Neymar Jr.

COLOR CRAFT

ColorCraftBooks.com

Table Of Contents

Claim Your Free Bonuses

There are three bonuses waiting for you as a thank you for picking up this book:

🏆 **Exclusive Bonus Biography** of a surprise superstar. *Who will it be?* 👀

✨ **Sports Star Trivia Pack** with 25 questions about famous athletes: *can you guess the answers?*

🚀 **Sports Challenge Activity Sheet** with 9 sports real-life sports challenges. *Can you complete them all?*

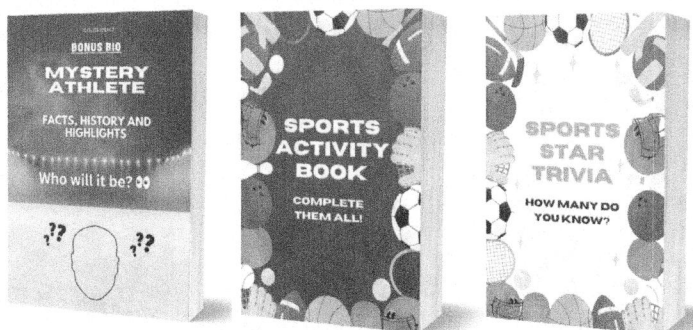

Just scan the QR code below or visit

bonus.colorcraftbooks.com/sports.

Scan to download. Kids: be sure to ask a parent first! ⬤

Collect Them All: Our Exciting Bios for Kids

Steph Curry

Anthony Edwards

Victor Wembanyama

Luka Dončić

Simone Biles

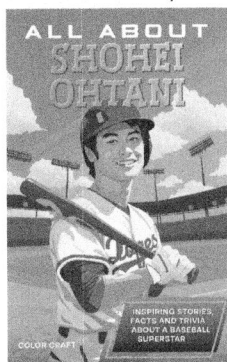
Shohei Ohtani

Leo Messi

Neymar Jr.

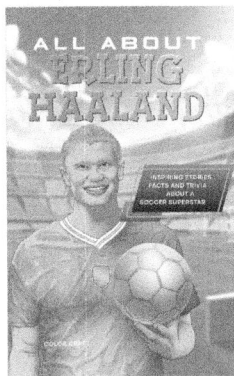
Erling Haaland

Find them on Amazon by visiting ColorCraftBooks.com/books.

Introduction: The Electrifying Goal: Neymar Jr.'s Stunning Hat-Trick

In the world of soccer, some moments become legendary. One such moment in Neymar Jr.'s career took place during an unforgettable Champions League match that left fans breathless and his opponents in awe.

It was a night that showcased his incredible talent, determination, and flair for the dramatic—a night that would be talked about for years to come.

The stadium buzzed with excitement as thousands of fans filled the seats, waving flags and chanting in unison. The atmosphere was electric, and the stakes were high. Neymar Jr.'s team needed a miracle to advance to the next round of the tournament.

They were down by three goals, and the odds were stacked against them. But Neymar Jr., known for his never-give-up attitude, was ready to give it his all.

From the moment the referee blew the whistle, Neymar Jr. was unstoppable. He darted across the field with the speed and agility of a cheetah, his eyes locked on the ball.

His first goal came in the 50th minute—a stunning strike from outside the penalty box that sailed past the goalkeeper and into the top corner of the net. The crowd erupted in cheers, and hope flickered in the hearts of his teammates and fans.

But Neymar Jr. wasn't done yet. Just ten minutes later, he dribbled past three defenders with dazzling footwork that left them stumbling.

As he approached the goal, he took a quick glance at the goalkeeper's position and expertly chipped the ball over his head.

The ball floated gracefully into the net, and the stadium roared with applause. Neymar Jr. had brought his team within one goal of tying the game.

The clock was ticking down, and the tension was palpable. With only minutes left, Neymar Jr. received a pass from a teammate near the corner flag.

He skillfully controlled the ball and drove toward the goal, determined to complete his hat-trick. The defenders closed in on him, but Neymar Jr. remained calm and focused.

With a swift movement, he flicked the ball over their heads, sprinted around them, and volleyed it into the back of the net.

The stadium erupted into a frenzy of cheers, chants, and celebrations. Neymar Jr. had done the impossible—he had scored a hat-trick in the most critical moment of the game, bringing his team level and sending the match into extra time.

His teammates mobbed him, lifting him into the air as fans chanted his name. It was a moment of pure joy, triumph, and inspiration.

In extra time, Neymar Jr.'s team went on to score the winning goal, securing their place in the next round of the tournament.

The victory was a testament to Neymar Jr.'s incredible skill, determination, and ability to perform under pressure. It was a night that showcased why he was considered one of the best soccer players in the world.

But beyond the goals and the glory, what made this moment truly special was Neymar Jr.'s unwavering belief in himself and his team. He had faced countless challenges and obstacles throughout his career, but he never gave up. His passion for the game, his relentless work ethic, and his love for his fans drove him to achieve greatness.

This stunning hat-trick was more than just a soccer achievement—it was a symbol of perseverance, resilience, and the power of believing in oneself. It inspired countless young fans around the world to chase their dreams and never give up, no matter how difficult the journey might be.

Neymar Jr.'s journey to this incredible moment wasn't easy. He had faced injuries, tough losses, and moments of doubt. But each setback only fueled his determination to come back stronger.

As we dive into the life and career of Neymar Jr., we'll explore the moments that shaped him, the challenges he overcame, and the victories that made him a global icon.

From his early days kicking a soccer ball in Brazil to becoming a superstar on the world stage.

So, get ready to be inspired by the incredible journey of Neymar Jr.—a soccer legend whose electrifying performances continue to captivate fans and inspire young athletes everywhere.

This is the story of a boy with big dreams who grew up to become one of the most exciting and beloved soccer players in the world.

And it all started with a ball, a dream, and a belief in himself.

Chapter 1: Meet Neymar Jr.: Soccer's Superhero

"The secret is to believe in your dreams; in your potential that you can be like your star, keep searching, keep believing, and don't lose faith in yourself." - Neymar Jr.

Neymar Jr. isn't just a soccer player; he's a global superstar, a magician with the ball, and an inspiration to millions of fans worldwide.

His journey from the streets of Brazil to the grand stadiums of Europe is a testament to his talent, hard work, and unyielding passion for the game.

So, what makes Neymar Jr. so special?

Why is he regarded as one of the best soccer players in the world?

Neymar Jr.'s skill with the ball is unparalleled. From a young age, he showcased a natural talent for soccer that set him apart from his peers.

His dribbling skills are legendary, allowing him to weave through defenders with ease, making it seem like the ball is glued to his feet.

Fans are mesmerized by his fancy footwork, tricks, and flicks that leave opponents bewildered and spectators in awe. Neymar Jr. makes the game look effortless and fun, drawing people to his matches.

Did you know:

FOND OF TATTOOS

Neymar Jr. has a deep love for tattoos. Each of his tattoos has a special meaning, representing his family, faith, and career. For example, he has a tattoo of his sister Rafaella's face on his arm, showing their close bond.

But Neymar Jr.'s appeal isn't just about his skills. His charisma and personality, both on and off the field, make him a beloved figure. He plays with joy and enthusiasm, celebrating goals with energy and happiness that spread smiles among fans and teammates.

His bright smile and positive attitude make him a role model for young fans everywhere.

Neymar Jr. is also incredibly versatile on the field. Whether playing as a forward, winger, or attacking midfielder, his speed and agility allow him to change directions effortlessly, making it difficult for defenders to keep up.

His ability to score goals, create assists, and make game-changing plays has earned him a reputation as a game-changer.

Another reason Neymar Jr. has become a star is his impressive track record.

He has played for some of the biggest clubs in the world, including Barcelona and Paris Saint-Germain, where he has won numerous titles and accolades.

From league championships to prestigious tournaments like the Champions League, Neymar Jr. has consistently performed at the highest level.

His individual awards, such as being named the South American Footballer of the Year multiple times, underscore his extraordinary talent and dedication.

Did you know:

FAMILY TRADITION

Soccer runs in Neymar Jr.'s family. His father, Neymar Santos Sr., was also a professional soccer player and has been a significant influence in Neymar Jr.'s career, providing guidance and support throughout his journey.

Beyond soccer, Neymar Jr. is known for his philanthropic efforts and community work. Despite his success, he hasn't forgotten his roots. He has used his fame and resources to give back, supporting various charitable causes and helping those in need.

His work with the Neymar Jr. Institute, which provides education and sports opportunities to underprivileged children in Brazil, showcases his commitment to making a positive difference in the world.

Despite his achievements, Neymar Jr. has faced challenges and setbacks. Injuries, criticism, and intense pressure are part of any professional athlete's life, and Neymar Jr. is no exception.

However, his resilience and determination to overcome these obstacles have made him stronger. He always comes back from setbacks with renewed vigor, proving that true champions never give up.

One of the most inspiring aspects of Neymar Jr.'s journey is his unwavering belief in himself and his dreams.

From playing soccer in the streets of Mogi das Cruzes, Brazil, to becoming a professional soccer player, Neymar Jr. pursued his passion with relentless dedication. His story is a powerful reminder that with hard work, perseverance, and self-belief, anything is possible.

Neymar Jr. has also become a global ambassador for soccer, promoting the sport to new audiences.

His influence extends to social media, where he connects with millions of fans, sharing glimpses of his life, training, and matches.

His vibrant personality and style have made him a favorite among fans of all ages.

Next up: Let's see where it all started for Neymar Jr.

Chapter 2: Kicking Off: Neymar's Childhood Dreams

"There is no pressure when you are making a dream come true." - Neymar Jr.

Neymar Jr.'s story begins in Mogi das Cruzes, a bustling city in Brazil. Born on February 5, 1992, his full name is Neymar da Silva Santos Júnior, grew up in a loving family that played a significant role in shaping his future.

His father, Neymar Santos Sr., was a former soccer player who recognized his son's talent early on.

His mother, Nadine da Silva, provided the support and encouragement that helped Neymar Jr. chase his dreams.

From the moment he could walk, Neymar Jr. had a soccer ball at his feet. He played soccer in the streets, parks, and any open space he could find. The narrow alleyways of his neighborhood became his first soccer field, and his friends were his first teammates.

These early games were not just fun for young Neymar; they were the beginning of his journey to becoming a soccer superstar.

Growing up in Brazil, soccer was more than just a sport—it was a way of life. Neymar Jr. idolized famous Brazilian players like Pelé and Ronaldinho, dreaming of one day becoming like them.

He watched their games on TV, mimicking their moves and imagining himself on the grand stage. These dreams fueled his passion and dedication to the sport.

Did you know:

MULTILINGUAL SKILLS

Neymar Jr. speaks multiple languages fluently, including Portuguese, Spanish, and English. This ability has helped him adapt quickly to different teams and communicate effectively with teammates and coaches from various countries.

Life was not always easy for Neymar Jr. and his family. They faced financial struggles, and there were times when money was tight.

Despite these challenges, his family always supported his love for soccer. His father took on various jobs to provide for the family and ensure Neymar Jr. had everything he needed to pursue his passion.

Their sacrifices and hard work laid the foundation for his future success.Neymar Jr. also had a younger sister, Rafaella, who was his biggest fan and supporter.

The bond between them was strong, and they often played together. Neymar Jr.'s family was his anchor, providing him with the love and stability he needed to focus on his dreams.

As Neymar Jr. grew older, his talent became more evident. By the age of six, he was already playing for local teams and showing skills far beyond his years.

His father coached him, teaching him the fundamentals of the game and sharing his own experiences as a player.

These early lessons were invaluable, shaping Neymar Jr.'s understanding of soccer and helping him develop his unique style of play.

One significant event in Neymar Jr.'s childhood was joining the Portuguesa Santista youth team at the age of seven. This was a big step for him, as it marked the beginning of his formal training.

At Portuguesa Santista, Neymar Jr. honed his skills, learned teamwork, and faced tougher competition. His talent quickly caught the attention of scouts and coaches, who saw great potential in the young player.

Despite his natural ability, Neymar Jr. faced challenges on his journey. The competition was fierce, and there were times when he doubted himself.

But with the support of his family and his unwavering determination, he pushed through these difficulties. He practiced tirelessly, always striving to improve and prove himself on the field.

Did you know:

LOVES COMIC BOOKS

Neymar Jr. is a huge fan of comic books, especially those featuring superheroes like Spider-Man and Batman. He has even incorporated his love for these characters into his personal style, often wearing clothing and accessories adorned with superhero logos.

Another pivotal moment in Neymar Jr.'s early life was his move to Santos FC's youth academy when he was just eleven years old. This move was both exciting and challenging, as it meant leaving behind his friends and familiar surroundings.

But Neymar Jr. was ready for the challenge. At Santos FC, he was surrounded by talented players and top-notch coaches who helped him take his game to the next level.

During his time at Santos FC's youth academy, Neymar Jr. continued to impress everyone with his skills, speed, and creativity on the field.

He became known for his dribbling, precise passes, and ability to score goals from almost any position. His performances earned him a reputation as one of the most promising young players in Brazil.

Neymar Jr.'s early life was filled with both joys and challenges. The support of his family, his father's guidance, and his own determination helped him overcome obstacles and stay focused on his dreams.

These formative years shaped him into the player and person he would become, instilling in him a strong work ethic, resilience, and a love for the game that would drive him to greatness.

As we think about Neymar Jr.'s early life, it's clear that his journey wasn't just about his amazing talent. It was also about the people who believed in him and the tough times that made him stronger.

From playing soccer in the streets of Mogi das Cruzes to training at Santos FC, Neymar Jr.'s childhood dreams built the path for his incredible career.

His story shows us that with passion, hard work, and support from loved ones, even the biggest dreams can come true.

Chapter 3: Young Prodigy: The Making of a Star

"I just like winning every tournament that I play. All of them are important for me. Each has its own history, its own characteristic, but they are all important." - Neymar Jr.

Neymar Jr.'s journey from a talented child to a budding soccer star began when he joined the youth academy at Santos FC around the age of ten.

From ages 10 to 16, this period was crucial in shaping him into the phenomenal player he is today. It was filled with hard work, dedication, and overcoming challenges that tested his resolve.

At Santos FC, Neymar Jr. faced intense competition. The other young players were equally talented and driven, each vying for a spot on the team and the attention of the coaches.

This environment pushed Neymar Jr. to work harder and refine his skills.

He spent countless hours practicing dribbling, passing, and shooting, always striving to improve. His natural talent, combined with his relentless work ethic, set him apart from the rest.

Did you know:

FOCUSED DIET
To maintain his top physical condition, Neymar Jr. follows a strict diet plan. He focuses on eating balanced meals that include lean proteins, whole grains, and plenty of fruits and vegetables. This diet helps him stay fit and ready for the demands of professional soccer.

One significant challenge Neymar Jr. faced during this time was managing the pressure of expectations. As his reputation grew, so did the expectations of his coaches, teammates, and fans.

The pressure to perform could have been overwhelming, but Neymar Jr. thrived under it. He developed mental toughness, focusing on his love for the game and his desire to be the best.

During these years, Neymar Jr. also had to balance his education with soccer. His family valued schooling, and Neymar Jr. worked hard to ensure he didn't fall behind in his studies.

This balancing act required discipline and time management, skills he would continue to use throughout his life.

Two key figures played a pivotal role in Neymar Jr.'s development during this period: his father, Neymar Santos Sr., and his coach at Santos FC, Betinho.

Neymar Santos Sr.: The Guiding Hand

Neymar Jr.'s father, Neymar Santos Sr., was more than just a parent; he was his mentor, coach, and biggest supporter.

A former soccer player himself, Neymar Sr. understood the demands of the sport and the sacrifices required to succeed.

He guided Neymar Jr. through the ups and downs, providing advice, encouragement, and tough love when needed. Neymar Sr. often trained with him outside of formal practice sessions, teaching him discipline, hard work, and humility.

Betinho: The Inspirational Coach

At Santos FC, Neymar Jr. was coached by Betinho, a highly respected figure in Brazilian youth soccer.

Betinho recognized Neymar Jr.'s potential early on and took him under his wing.

He focused on developing Neymar Jr.'s technical abilities and nurturing his mental and emotional growth. Betinho encouraged Neymar Jr. to express himself on the field, helping him develop his signature flair and confidence.

Under Betinho's guidance, Neymar Jr. learned valuable lessons about teamwork, sportsmanship, and leadership. Betinho emphasized the importance of working with teammates, respecting opponents, and staying grounded despite success.

One of the most memorable moments during this period was Neymar Jr.'s debut for the Santos FC senior team at the age of 15.

It was a dream come true and marked the beginning of his professional career. Despite his youth, Neymar Jr. displayed maturity and composure on the field, impressing both his teammates and coaches.

Did you know:

FAVORITE FOOD

Neymar Jr.'s favorite food is pizza. He loves trying different types of pizza from around the world, and it's his go-to meal after a big game. He often shares his pizza adventures with fans on social media.

However, the road to success was not without obstacles. Neymar Jr. faced injuries that temporarily sidelined him and tested his resilience. Each time, he worked diligently on his recovery, returning to the field stronger and more determined.

These experiences taught him the importance of perseverance and maintaining a positive mindset, even in the face of adversity.

As Neymar Jr. continued to develop, his performances caught the attention of scouts and soccer enthusiasts worldwide. His unique combination of speed, skill, and creativity made him a rising star in Brazilian soccer. By the time he was 16, Neymar Jr. was already being compared to some of the greatest players in the sport, and his future looked incredibly bright.

Neymar Jr.'s journey from a young hopeful to a rising star was a testament to his talent, hard work, and the unwavering support of his family and mentors.

The challenges he overcame and the lessons he learned during this period laid the foundation for his future success. His story is an inspiration to young athletes everywhere, showing that with dedication, resilience, and the right guidance, dreams can come true.

As we look back on Neymar Jr.'s early development, we see that these years were crucial in shaping him into the player and person he is today.

The support of his father, the mentorship of Coach Betinho, and his own drive helped him navigate the challenges and seize the opportunities that came his way.

This period of Neymar Jr.'s life is a reminder that great things don't happen overnight but through years of hard work, perseverance, and passion for the game.

Chapter 4: Teen Sensation: Neymar's Rise to Fame

"I'm always happy. In every game and every win, I keep writing my history, and I hope to do even more from now on." - Neymar Jr.

Neymar Jr.'s early career was filled with incredible achievements and a rapid rise to fame. From the age of 16, he began to make waves in the world of soccer, showing everyone, he was not just a talented youngster but a prodigy destined for greatness.

At just 16, Neymar Jr. was already playing for the senior team of Santos FC, one of Brazil's top soccer clubs. On March 7, 2009, he stepped onto the field for the first time as a professional player.

Despite his youth, Neymar Jr. displayed remarkable composure and skill, impressing fans and critics alike. This debut match was just a glimpse of the brilliance that was to come.

One of Neymar Jr.'s standout achievements during his early career was winning the Campeonato Paulista with Santos FC.

In 2010, just a year after his debut, he played a crucial role in helping his team secure the title. His exceptional dribbling, quick footwork, and goal-scoring ability made him a standout player.

This victory was just the beginning of a series of successes that would define his early career.

In the same year, Neymar Jr. was awarded the prestigious "Best Young Player" title by the Brazilian Football Confederation.

This award recognized his outstanding performances and his potential to become one of the best players in the world. Winning this award at such a young age was a testament to his hard work, dedication, and natural talent.

As Neymar Jr.'s reputation grew, so did the media attention surrounding him. He quickly became a household name in Brazil, with fans eagerly following his every move.

Nationally televised games featuring Neymar Jr. drew huge audiences, and his matches became must-watch events. His charismatic personality and flair for the dramatic made him a favorite among commentators and fans alike.

Did you know:

FASHION ICON

Neymar Jr. is known for his unique and trendy fashion sense. He often collaborates with top fashion brands and designers, showcasing his style both on and off the field. His bold fashion choices have made him a style icon for many fans around the world.

Neymar Jr.'s rise to fame also caught the attention of international scouts and clubs. Major European teams began to take notice of the young Brazilian, recognizing his potential to become a global superstar. This interest from abroad added to the excitement and anticipation surrounding his career.

In 2011, Neymar Jr. led Santos FC to victory in the Copa Libertadores, one of the most prestigious club tournaments in South America. This victory was particularly significant because it marked Santos FC's first Copa Libertadores title since the days of Pelé, the legendary Brazilian soccer player.

Neymar Jr.'s performances in the tournament were nothing short of spectacular. He scored key goals, delivered decisive assists, and showcased his ability to perform under pressure.

Neymar Jr.'s success in the Copa Libertadores brought him even more fame and recognition. He was named the "Best Player" of the tournament, an honor that further solidified his status as a rising star.

This achievement also increased his visibility on the global stage, with fans and clubs from around the world paying close attention to his career.

During this time, Neymar Jr. also became a popular figure in the media. He appeared on the covers of numerous sports magazines, was featured in television interviews, and became a regular topic of discussion on sports shows.

His style, both on and off the field, made him a trendsetter. His hairstyles, fashion choices, and vibrant personality attracted a large following, especially among young fans.

One of the most memorable moments in Neymar Jr.'s early career was his goal against Flamengo in 2011, which was later awarded the FIFA Puskás Award for the best goal of the year. In this match, Neymar Jr. dribbled past several defenders with dazzling skill and speed before calmly slotting the ball into the net.

This goal was a perfect example of his creativity, technical ability, and confidence. It became an iconic moment in his career and a highlight that is still celebrated by fans today.

As Neymar Jr. continued to excel on the field, his fame reached new heights. He became a global ambassador for Brazilian soccer, representing his country in international tournaments and friendlies.

His performances for the Brazilian national team further showcased his talent and solidified his place among the best young players in the world.

By the age of 18, Neymar Jr. had already achieved more than many players do in their entire careers.

His journey from a promising youth player to a teenage sensation was marked by hard work, resilience, and a relentless pursuit of excellence. He had faced challenges and pressure but had risen above them with grace and determination.

Neymar Jr.'s early career was not just about individual achievements; it was also about inspiring a new generation of soccer players. His success showed young athletes around the world that dreams could come true with dedication, passion, and perseverance.

He became a role model, encouraging kids to believe in themselves and pursue their goals, no matter how big.

As we look back on Neymar Jr.'s early career, it's clear that his journey was filled with amazing talent and unstoppable commitment.

From winning big titles and awards to thrilling fans with his incredible skills and charm, Neymar Jr. set the stage for an even more fantastic future. His story shows us how powerful dreams, hard work, and believing in yourself can be.

Neymar Jr.'s rise to fame was like a rollercoaster of achievements, media buzz, and unforgettable moments.

This was when the world first saw the making of a soccer legend—a player who would leave a lasting mark on the sport and inspire millions around the world.

Chapter 5: World Stage: Neymar Takes Over Soccer

"I always do as my heart tells me." - Neymar Jr.

As Neymar Jr. entered his twenties, he embarked on a journey that would see him become one of the greatest soccer players of his generation.

This period marked the prime of his career, filled with incredible achievements, jaw-dropping performances, and inspiring moments that captivated fans around the world.

In 2013, at just 21 years old, Neymar Jr. made a monumental move to FC Barcelona, one of the most prestigious soccer clubs in the world.

This transfer was a dream come true for Neymar Jr., and it was one of the most talked-about deals in soccer history. The move to Barcelona was valued at €57 million, making it one of the largest transfers at the time. It was clear that Neymar Jr. was destined for greatness.

Playing alongside legends like Lionel Messi and Andrés Iniesta, Neymar Jr. became part of a formidable attacking trio known as "MSN" (Messi, Suárez, Neymar).

This trio wreaked havoc on defenses, combining their skills to create one of the most lethal attacking forces in soccer history. Their chemistry on the field was magical, leading Barcelona to numerous victories.

Did you know:

BIG ON SOCIAL MEDIA

Neymar Jr. is one of the most-followed athletes on social media. He has millions of followers on platforms like Instagram, Twitter, and Facebook. He uses these platforms to share his life, connect with fans, and promote his charitable initiatives.

In 2015, Neymar Jr. achieved one of his most significant milestones by winning the UEFA Champions League with Barcelona. This prestigious tournament is the pinnacle of club soccer in Europe, and winning it was a testament to Neymar Jr.'s talent and hard work.

He played a crucial role in the final, scoring a goal and providing an assist in a thrilling 3-1 victory against Juventus. Overcoming injuries and setbacks, he had risen to the top and achieved one of his biggest dreams.

That same year, Neymar Jr. and Barcelona also secured the treble, winning the La Liga, Copa del Rey, and UEFA Champions League titles in a single season. This remarkable achievement cemented their status as one of the greatest teams in soccer history.

Neymar Jr.'s contributions were invaluable, and he earned praise from fans, teammates, and coaches alike.

Neymar Jr.'s rise to prominence also included impressive individual honors. He consistently ranked among the top players in the world, finishing as a finalist for the FIFA Ballon d'Or, an award given to the best player in the world.

Although he didn't win the award during his time at Barcelona, his nominations were a testament to his incredible performances and the respect he earned in the soccer community.

In 2017, Neymar Jr. made headlines once again with a historic transfer to Paris Saint-Germain (PSG) in France.

The transfer fee of €222 million shattered the previous record, making Neymar Jr. the most expensive player in soccer history. This move was a bold step, showcasing Neymar Jr.'s ambition to take on new challenges and continue his journey of greatness.

Did you know:

MUSIC PASSION

Music plays a big role in Neymar Jr.'s life. He loves listening to various genres, especially samba and hip-hop. He often shares his favorite playlists with fans and sometimes even plays the piano in his free time.

At PSG, Neymar Jr. continued to shine, leading his team to multiple Ligue 1 titles, French Cups, and Super Cups. His impact on the field was undeniable, as he dazzled fans with his dribbling, scoring, and playmaking abilities. Despite facing injuries that sidelined him at times,

Neymar Jr. showed incredible resilience, always coming back stronger and more determined.

One of the most inspiring aspects of Neymar Jr.'s career was his ability to overcome adversity. He faced several significant injuries, including a broken foot that required surgery and lengthy rehabilitation.

Each time, Neymar Jr. demonstrated his mental toughness and dedication, working tirelessly to recover and return to peak form. His perseverance in the face of setbacks inspired many young athletes to never give up, no matter the challenges.

Neymar Jr. also experienced heartbreak in international tournaments with the Brazilian national team. In the 2014 FIFA World Cup, held in Brazil, he suffered a severe back injury in the quarterfinals, preventing him from playing in the rest of the tournament.

Brazil went on to suffer a devastating loss in the semifinals. However, Neymar Jr. bounced back in the 2016 Olympics, leading Brazil to its first-ever Olympic gold medal in soccer.

His decisive penalty kick in the final against Germany was a moment of redemption and joy for both Neymar Jr. and his country.

Throughout his career, Neymar Jr. developed rivalries with other top players and teams. Matches against Real Madrid, led by Cristiano Ronaldo, were always highly anticipated, pitting two of the best players in the world against each other.

These clashes were thrilling and showcased Neymar Jr.'s competitive spirit and ability to perform under pressure.

With such success, Neymar Jr. became a global icon, signing major sponsorship deals with brands like Nike, Red Bull, and Panasonic.

These partnerships highlighted his popularity and influence, allowing him to inspire young fans worldwide. While his family never stopped providing unwavering support and guidance throughout his career. Let's explore more about Neymar's life off the field.

Chapter 6: Beyond the Field: Neymar's Life Off the Pitch

"Our objective is always to win. Every day, every game, and every competition." - Neymar Jr.

Neymar Jr. is not just a superstar on the soccer field; he is also an incredible person off the pitch. His personality, family life, charitable work, and involvement in various ventures make him a well-rounded and inspiring figure for fans around the world. Let's take a closer look at Neymar Jr.'s life away from the professional arena and the many ways he has made a positive impact beyond soccer.

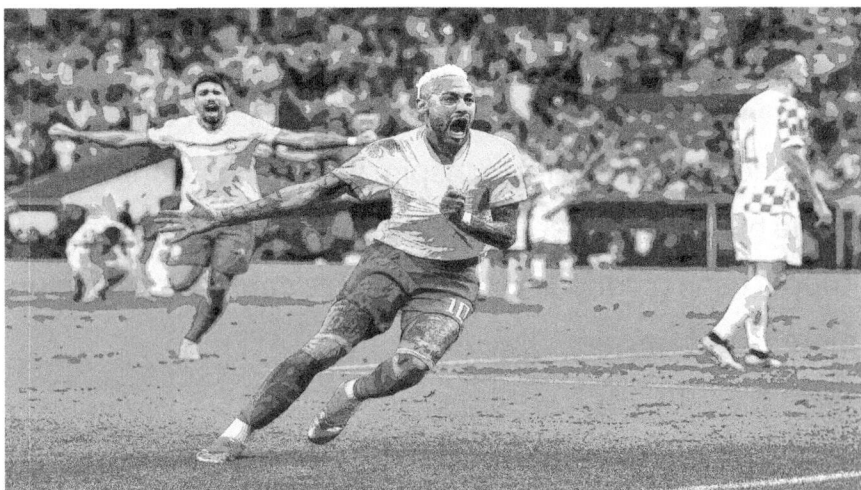

One of the most heartwarming aspects of Neymar Jr.'s life is his close-knit family. He has a son, Davi Lucca, who was born in 2011. Neymar Jr. is a devoted father, often sharing adorable moments with Davi on social media.

Whether they're playing soccer together, enjoying vacations, or simply spending quality time, it's clear that Neymar Jr. cherishes his role as a dad.

His love and dedication to his son are evident, and he strives to be a positive role model in Davi's life.

Did you know:

FLAMENCO DANCER
Besides soccer, Neymar Jr. has a talent for dancing. He has shown off his skills in flamenco, a traditional Spanish dance. This helps him with his footwork on the soccer field, making his movements even more fluid and graceful.

Neymar Jr.'s family extends beyond his son. He shares a special bond with his sister, Rafaella, who has been his biggest supporter from the start. The two siblings are very close, and Neymar Jr. often expresses his love and appreciation for Rafaella through social media posts and public appearances.

Their strong relationship is a testament to the importance of family in Neymar Jr.'s life.

In addition to his family, Neymar Jr. has a warm and joyful personality that shines both on and off the field. Known for his playful demeanor, he often celebrates his goals with dance moves, infectious laughter, and big smiles. His exuberant celebrations bring joy to fans and teammates alike, creating a positive and fun atmosphere during matches.

Neymar Jr.'s love for the game is evident in every match he plays, and his joyful spirit is one of the many reasons fans adore him.

Beyond his playful personality, Neymar Jr. is also known for his generous heart and dedication to giving back to the community.

He established the Neymar Jr. Institute, a non-profit organization that provides education, sports opportunities, and healthcare to underprivileged children in Brazil.

The institute, located in Praia Grande, aims to create a positive impact on the lives of thousands of young people, giving them hope and opportunities for a brighter future.

Did you know:

SUPPORTS CHARITIES

Neymar Jr. is deeply involved in charitable work. He established the Neymar Jr. Institute, which provides education, sports, and healthcare to underprivileged children in Brazil. He also supports various other charities, such as UNICEF, and other initiatives aimed at fighting poverty and promoting education.

Neymar Jr.'s charitable efforts go beyond his own foundation. He has supported various causes and participated in numerous charity events.

For example, he has been involved in initiatives to raise funds for children with cancer, supported disaster relief efforts, and contributed to campaigns aimed at fighting poverty and inequality.

His commitment to helping those in need showcases his compassionate nature and desire to make a difference in the world.

Did you know:

PET LOVER
Neymar Jr. is an animal lover and has several pets, including dogs named Poker and Truco. He often shares photos and videos of his pets on social media, showing his playful side off the field.

Outside of soccer, Neymar Jr. has ventured into various media and entertainment projects. He has made cameo appearances in movies, starred in commercials, and even tried his hand at music.

His ventures into entertainment highlight his versatility and ability to connect with fans in different ways.

Neymar Jr. has also been featured on the covers of numerous magazines, including prestigious publications like Time and Sports Illustrated.

These features often highlight his impact on and off the field, celebrating his achievements and contributions to society. His charismatic personality and global influence have made him a sought-after figure for interviews, podcasts, and television appearances.

Throughout his career, Neymar Jr. has received numerous honors and accolades. In addition to his soccer awards, he has been recognized for his charitable work and contributions to the community.

For instance, he was named a UNESCO Champion for Peace, an honor that acknowledges his efforts to promote education, sports, and peace around the world. This recognition is a testament to Neymar Jr.'s dedication to using his platform for positive change.

Did you know:

SKATEBOARDING HOBBY

Skateboarding is one of Neymar Jr.'s favorite pastimes. He enjoys the thrill and challenge of performing tricks and often uses it as a way to relax and have fun when he's not playing soccer.

Neymar Jr. has also had the privilege of meeting influential figures and world leaders.

After winning the 2016 Olympic gold medal, he and his teammates were honored by the Brazilian government.

Neymar Jr. had the opportunity to meet the country's president. These moments of recognition and celebration highlight the impact of his achievements and the pride he brings to his nation.

Neymar Jr.'s life beyond soccer is filled with love, joy, and a commitment to making the world a better place.

His close relationship with his family, playful personality, and generous heart have made him popular with fans all over the world.

Chapter 7: Record Breaker: Neymar's Achievements and Legacy

"I am not the type of person who lets the pressure get to him. I try to see it as my friend. I align with it to calm me down." - Neymar Jr.

Neymar Jr. has accomplished incredible feats throughout his career, establishing himself as one of the greatest soccer players of his generation. From winning prestigious tournaments to setting records, his journey is filled with remarkable achievements that inspire young athletes around the world. Let's dive into some of the highlights of Neymar Jr.'s illustrious career.

Winning the UEFA Champions League

One of Neymar Jr.'s most significant achievements came in 2015 when he won the UEFA Champions League with FC Barcelona. This tournament is the most prestigious club competition in Europe, and lifting the trophy is a dream for any soccer player. Neymar Jr. played a crucial role in

Barcelona's success, scoring key goals and providing assists throughout the tournament.

In the final against Juventus, Neymar Jr. scored a goal in the dying moments of the game, sealing a 3-1 victory for Barcelona. This triumph was a testament to his talent and dedication, marking one of the highest points in his career.

Did you know:

VIDEO GAME ENTHUSIAST
Neymar Jr. loves playing video games, especially FIFA and Call of Duty. He often plays online with friends and fans, and even participates in gaming tournaments. This hobby allows him to connect with fans and relax after intense training sessions.

The Treble with Barcelona

In the same year, Neymar Jr. and his teammates at Barcelona achieved the incredible feat of winning the treble.

This means they won three major trophies in one season: La Liga (the Spanish league), Copa del Rey (the Spanish cup), and the UEFA Champions League. This historic accomplishment showcased Neymar Jr.'s ability to perform at the highest level and his importance to the team's success.

His contributions on the field were vital in securing these titles, and this achievement is celebrated by fans and soccer enthusiasts alike.

Olympic Gold Medal

Representing Brazil, Neymar Jr. led his national team to victory in the 2016 Olympics held in Rio de Janeiro. This tournament was especially meaningful for Neymar Jr. and the Brazilian people. In the final match against Germany, Neymar Jr. scored a stunning free-kick goal and later netted the winning penalty in the shootout, securing Brazil's first-ever Olympic gold medal in soccer.

This moment of triumph was a symbol of resilience and determination, and it cemented Neymar Jr.'s legacy as a national hero. The victory brought immense joy to the country and is considered one of the most memorable moments in Brazilian soccer history.

Copa Libertadores Victory

Before his move to Europe, Neymar Jr. achieved significant success with Santos FC in Brazil. In 2011, he led Santos to victory in the Copa Libertadores, the most prestigious club tournament in South America. This win was particularly special because it marked Santos FC's first Copa Libertadores title since the days of Pelé.

Neymar Jr.'s performances in the tournament were nothing short of spectacular. He scored key goals, delivered decisive assists, and showcased his ability to perform under pressure. Winning the Copa Libertadores was a major milestone in his career and demonstrated his potential to succeed on the global stage.

FIFA Puskás Award

In 2011, Neymar Jr. received the FIFA Puskás Award for the best goal of the year. This prestigious award recognized his incredible goal against Flamengo, where he dribbled past several defenders with dazzling skill and speed before calmly slotting the ball into the net.

This goal was a perfect example of his creativity, technical ability, and confidence. It became an iconic moment in his career and a highlight that is still celebrated by fans today. Winning the Puskás Award was a testament to Neymar Jr.'s talent and his ability to create moments of magic on the field.

Top Scorer Titles

Throughout his career, Neymar Jr. has consistently been one of the top scorers in the leagues he has played in. Whether it was in Brazil, Spain, or France, he has always had a knack for finding the back of the net.

His goal-scoring prowess has earned him multiple top scorer titles, including the Campeonato Paulista top scorer in 2010, the Copa do Brasil top scorer in 2010, and the Ligue 1 top scorer in the 2017-2018 season. These achievements highlight his consistency and ability to perform at the highest level year after year.

Participation in All-Star Games

Neymar Jr. has been invited to participate in various all-star games and special matches throughout his career.

These events bring together the best players from around the world, showcasing their skills in a fun and competitive environment. Neymar Jr.'s inclusion in these games is a testament to his status as one of the top players in the world. Fans enjoy watching him compete against other soccer stars, and his performances in these games are always exciting and entertaining.

Statistics and Records Neymar Jr.'s career is filled with impressive statistics and records that highlight his impact on the game. Here are some of the most notable:

- **Goals Scored:** Neymar Jr. has scored over 470 career goals for club and country, showcasing his incredible goal-scoring ability.
- **Assists:** He has provided over 280 assists, demonstrating his playmaking skills and ability to create opportunities for his teammates.

- **Hat-Tricks:** Neymar Jr. has scored over 20 hat-tricks (three goals in a single game) throughout his career, highlighting his ability to take over matches.
- **Youngest to Score 100 Goals for Santos:** At just 20 years old, Neymar Jr. became the youngest player to score 100 goals for Santos FC, a remarkable achievement that underscored his talent and potential.
- **Record Transfer Fee:** In 2017, Neymar Jr.'s transfer to Paris Saint-Germain (PSG) for €222 million shattered the previous record, making him the most expensive player in soccer history.

International Achievements

Neymar Jr. has represented Brazil in multiple FIFA World Cups, bringing pride and joy to his country. His performances in these tournaments have captivated fans worldwide, and he has consistently been one of the standout players. Despite facing injuries and setbacks, Neymar Jr.'s dedication to his national team and his desire to bring glory to Brazil have never wavered.

Sponsorship Deals and Endorsements Neymar Jr.'s success on the field has also led to numerous lucrative sponsorship deals and endorsements.

He has signed contracts with major brands like Nike, Red Bull, and Panasonic, becoming one of the highest-paid athletes in the world.

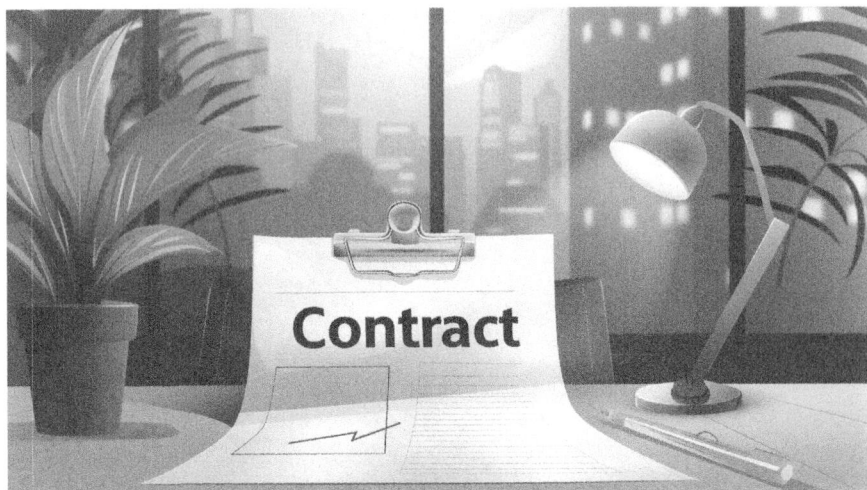

His contract with Nike, in particular, was one of the largest in sports history, highlighting his marketability and influence. These deals not only showcase his popularity but also allow him to use his platform to inspire young fans around the world.

Off the Field Honors Neymar Jr. has received numerous honors and accolades for his contributions to soccer and society. He was named a UNESCO Champion for Peace, an honor that acknowledges his efforts to promote education, sports, and peace around the world. This recognition is a testament to Neymar Jr.'s dedication to using his platform for positive change.

Neymar Jr.'s career is filled with extraordinary achievements, impressive statistics, and memorable moments. From winning prestigious tournaments and setting records to inspiring young athletes and giving back to the community, Neymar Jr. has left an unforgettable mark on the world of soccer.

His story speaks to the power of hard work, determination, and the belief that dreams can come true. Neymar Jr. continues to inspire us, showing young athletes that with passion and perseverance, anything is possible.

The Final Whistle: Neymar Jr.'s Legacy and Your Journey Ahead

As we reach the end of Neymar Jr.'s incredible journey, we've explored his life from a young soccer enthusiast in Brazil to becoming a global superstar. This book has taken you through Neymar Jr.'s early life, his rise to fame, and the numerous achievements that have defined his career. We've seen how his hard work, determination, and love for the game have propelled him to the top of the soccer world.

Neymar Jr.'s story is more than just a series of accomplishments. It's a testament to the power of dreams, perseverance, and the support of family and mentors.

His journey shows us that with passion, dedication, and resilience, we can overcome any obstacles and achieve our goals. Whether it's bouncing back from injuries, winning prestigious titles, or inspiring millions with his charitable work, Neymar Jr. has demonstrated that greatness is not just about talent but also about heart and character.

For all the young readers out there, remember that you, too, can achieve amazing things. Whether you dream of being a soccer star, an artist, a scientist, or anything else, the key is to believe in yourself, work hard, and never give up. Surround yourself with supportive people, stay positive, and keep pushing forward, no matter what challenges you face.

Thank you for joining us on this journey through Neymar Jr.'s life. We hope you've found his story as inspiring and exciting as we have. Keep chasing your dreams, and remember that every great achievement starts with a single step.

Don't forget the trivia section and timeline coming up next - test your knowledge, impress your friends and family, and see who knows the most about Neymar Jr.! Thank you for reading!

Neymar Jr. Trivia Challenge

Test your knowledge with these 30 trivia questions about Neymar Jr.! Choose the correct answer from the options provided for each question.

Many of these are contained in this book. Some aren't - so you might know them already, or you might learn something new.

Test yourself, test your family, and try these out on your friends to find out who the biggest Neymar Jr. Expert is!

The answers are at the end.

1. Where was Neymar Jr. born?

   A. Rio de Janeiro

   B. São Paulo

   C. Mogi das Cruzes

2. At what age did Neymar Jr. make his debut for Santos FC's senior team?

   A. 15

   B. 16

   C. 17

3. What is Neymar Jr.'s full name?

   A. Neymar Silva dos Santos Jr.

   B. Neymar da Silva Santos Júnior

   C. Neymar Santos da Silva Júnior

4. Which club did Neymar Jr. join in 2013?

   A. Real Madrid

   B. Paris Saint-Germain

   C. FC Barcelona

5. What year did Neymar Jr. win the UEFA Champions
   League with Barcelona?
   A. 2014
   B. 2015
   C. 2016

6. What nickname was given to the attacking trio of
   Messi, Suárez, and Neymar at Barcelona?
   A. MSN
   B. MNS
   C. SNM

7. Which tournament did Neymar Jr. help Brazil win its
   first gold medal in soccer?
   A. World Cup
    B. Copa America
   C. Olympics

8. How much was Neymar Jr.'s transfer fee to Paris Saint-Germain in 2017?

A. €150 million

B. €200 million

C. €222 million

9. What is the name of Neymar Jr.'s son?

A. David Lucca

B. Davi Lucca

C. Dani Lucca

10. Which year did Neymar Jr. receive the FIFA Puskás Award?

A. 2010

B. 2011

C. 2012

11. In which city did Neymar Jr. lead Brazil to Olympic gold in 2016?

A. Rio de Janeiro

B. São Paulo

C. Brasília

12. What position does Neymar Jr. primarily play?

    A. Goalkeeper

    B. Defender

    C. Forward

13. Who was Neymar Jr.'s coach at Santos FC?

    A. Betinho

    B. Tite

    C. Scolari

14. What major achievement did Neymar Jr. accomplish with Santos FC in 2011?

    A. Copa do Brasil

    B. Copa Libertadores

    C. Campeonato Brasileiro

15. How many goals has Neymar Jr. scored in his career (as of the book's publication)?

    A. Over 200 B.

    Over 300 C.

    Over 400

16. What year was Neymar Jr. born?

    A. 1990

    B. 1992

    C. 1994

17. What award did Neymar Jr. win in 2010 from the
    Brazilian Football Confederation?

    A. Best Player

    B. Best Young Player

    C. Top Scorer

18. Which brand has Neymar Jr. signed a major
    sponsorship deal with?
    A. Adidas
    B. Puma
    C. Nike

19. Who did Neymar Jr. score his first goal for PSG
    against?
    A. Marseille
    B. Toulouse
    C. Monaco

20.What was the name of the non-profit organization
    Neymar Jr. established?
    A. Neymar Foundation
    B. Neymar Jr. Institute
    C. Neymar Charity

21. Who are Neymar Jr.'s famous teammates at PSG?
    A. Cristiano Ronaldo and Lionel Messi
    B. Kylian Mbappé and Edinson Cavani
    C. Luka Modrić and Sergio Ramos

22. What major injury did Neymar Jr. suffer during the 2014 World Cup?
    A. Knee injury
    B. Back injury
    C. Ankle injury

23. What special goal celebration is Neymar Jr. known for?
    A. Backflip
    B. Dancing
    C. Somersault

24. What is Neymar Jr.'s sister's name?
    A. Rafaella
    B. Raquel
    C. Renata

25. Which year did Neymar Jr. lead Brazil to a Copa America victory?
    A. 2018
    B. 2019
    C. 2020

26. How many assists has Neymar Jr. provided in his career (as of the book's publication)?

A. Over 100 B.

Over 150 C.

Over 200

27. Which prestigious honor was Neymar Jr. named by UNESCO?

A. Champion for Peace

B. Global Ambassador for Sports

C. Humanitarian of the Year

28. In which year did Neymar Jr. score his iconic goal against Flamengo that won the FIFA Puskás Award?

A. 2010

B. 2011

C. 2012

29.How many times has Neymar Jr. finished as a
finalist for the FIFA Ballon d'Or?

A. Twice

B. Three times

C. Four times

30.What is Neymar Jr.'s preferred jersey number?

A. 7

B. 10

C. 11

Answers

1. **C - Mogi das Cruzes.** Neymar Jr. was born in Mogi
   das Cruzes, a city in Brazil.

2. **B - 16.** Neymar Jr. made his debut for Santos FC's
   senior team at the age of 16.

3. **B - Neymar da Silva Santos Júnior.** This is Neymar
   Jr.'s full name.

4. **C - FC Barcelona.** Neymar Jr. joined FC Barcelona in
   2013.

5. **B - 2015.** Neymar Jr. won the UEFA Champions League with Barcelona in 2015.

6. **A - MSN.** The attacking trio of Messi, Suárez, and Neymar was nicknamed "MSN."

7. **C - Olympics.** Neymar Jr. helped Brazil win its first Olympic gold medal in soccer in 2016.

8. **C - €222 million.** Neymar Jr.'s transfer to PSG was for a record-breaking €222 million.

9. **B - Davi Lucca.** Neymar Jr.'s son's name is Davi Lucca.

10. **B - 2011.** Neymar Jr. received the FIFA Puskás Award in 2011.

11. **A - Rio de Janeiro.** Neymar Jr. led Brazil to Olympic gold in 2016 in Rio de Janeiro.

12. **C - Forward.** Neymar Jr. primarily plays as a forward.

13. **A - Betinho.** Neymar Jr.'s coach at Santos FC was Betinho.

14. **B - Copa Libertadores.** Neymar Jr. helped Santos FC win the Copa Libertadores in 2011.

15. **C - Over 400.** Neymar Jr. has scored over 400 goals in his career.

16. **B - 1992.** Neymar Jr. was born in 1992.

17. **B - Best Young Player.** Neymar Jr. won the Best Young Player award in 2010.

18. **C - Nike.** Neymar Jr. has a major sponsorship deal with Nike.

19. **B - Toulouse.** Neymar Jr. scored his first goal for PSG against Toulouse.

20. **B - Neymar Jr. Institute.** The non-profit organization Neymar Jr. established is called the Neymar Jr. Institute.

21. **B - Kylian Mbappé and Edinson Cavani.** Neymar Jr.'s famous teammates at PSG include Kylian Mbappé and Edinson Cavani.

22. **B - Back injury.** Neymar Jr. suffered a back injury during the 2014 World Cup.

23. **B - Dancing.** Neymar Jr. is known for his dancing goal celebrations.

24. **A - Rafaella.** Neymar Jr.'s sister's name is Rafaella.

25. **B - 2019.** Neymar Jr. led Brazil to a Copa America victory in 2019.

26. **C - Over 200.** Neymar Jr. has provided over 200 assists in his career.

27. **A - Champion for Peace.** Neymar Jr. was named a UNESCO Champion for Peace.

28. **B - 2011.** Neymar Jr. scored his iconic goal against Flamengo in 2011, winning the FIFA Puskás Award.

29. **B - Three times.** Neymar Jr. has finished as a finalist for the FIFA Ballon d'Or three times.

30. **B - 10.** Neymar Jr.'s preferred jersey number is 10.

Timeline of Greatness

Here's a timeline of some of the most iconic, important, and influential milestones in Neymar Jr.'s life (so far!):

February 5, 1992 - Neymar da Silva Santos Júnior is born in Mogi das Cruzes, São Paulo, Brazil.

2003 - At age 11, Neymar Jr. joins the youth academy of Santos FC, one of Brazil's most famous soccer clubs.

March 7, 2009 - At just 17, Neymar Jr. makes his debut for Santos FC's senior team, showcasing his incredible talent.

August 15, 2010 - Neymar Jr. wins the Best Young Player award from the Brazilian Football Confederation, marking his rise as a soccer prodigy.

June 22, 2011 - He led Santos FC to victory in the Copa Libertadores, their first since Pelé's era, and won the tournament's Most Valuable Player award.

July 27, 2011 - Neymar Jr. scores a goal against Flamengo, later winning the FIFA Puskás Award for the best goal of the year.

June 3, 2013 - Neymar Jr. signs with FC Barcelona, joining one of the world's most prestigious soccer clubs.

July 4, 2014 - He helped Brazil reach the semifinals of the FIFA World Cup but suffered a serious back injury in the quarterfinals against Colombia.

June 6, 2015 - Neymar Jr. wins the UEFA Champions League with Barcelona, scoring a goal in the final against Juventus, contributing to Barcelona's treble-winning season.

August 20, 2016 - Neymar Jr. leads Brazil to its first-ever Olympic gold medal in soccer at the Rio de Janeiro Olympics, scoring the winning penalty in the final against Germany.

August 3, 2017 - Neymar Jr. transfers to Paris Saint-Germain (PSG) for a record-breaking €222 million, becoming the most expensive player in soccer history.

May 8, 2018 - In his first season with PSG, Neymar Jr. helps the team win the Ligue 1 title, Coupe de France, and Coupe de la Ligue.

June 6, 2018 - Neymar Jr. participates in the FIFA World Cup in Russia, leading Brazil to the quarterfinals.

August 23, 2020 - He continues to shine at PSG, leading the team to the UEFA Champions League final, although they are defeated by Bayern Munich.

May 8, 2021 - Neymar Jr. extends his contract with PSG, committing to the club until 2025, aiming to bring more titles to the French giants.

November 24, 2022 - Neymar Jr. represents Brazil in the FIFA World Cup in Qatar, further solidifying his status as a key player for his national team.

August 15, 2023 - Neymar Jr. signs with Al-Hilal SFC, a Saudi Arabian club, beginning a new chapter in his career.

December 9, 2023 - Neymar Jr. breaks Pelé's long-standing record to become Brazil's all-time top goal-scorer.

June 4, 2024 - Neymar Jr. leads Al-Hilal to victory in the Saudi Pro League, adding another national title to his illustrious career.

Neymar Jr.'s journey is a testament to his incredible talent, dedication, and love for the game. From his early days at Santos FC to his record-breaking transfer to PSG, he has consistently demonstrated why he is one of the best soccer players in the world.

His story inspires young athletes everywhere to chase their dreams and never give up.

Collect Them All: Our Exciting Bios for Kids

Steph Curry

Anthony Edwards

Victor Wembanyama

Luka Dončić

Simone Biles

Shohei Ohtani

Leo Messi

Neymar Jr.

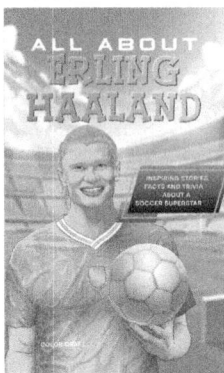

Erling Haaland

Find them on Amazon by visiting ColorCraftBooks.com/books.

Claim Your Free Bonuses

There are three bonuses waiting for you as a thank you for picking up this book:

🏆 **Exclusive Bonus Biography** of a surprise superstar. *Who will it be?* 👀

✦ **Sports Star Trivia Pack** with 25 questions about famous athletes: *can you guess the answers?*

🚀 **Sports Challenge Activity Sheet** with 9 sports real-life sports challenges. *Can you complete them all?*

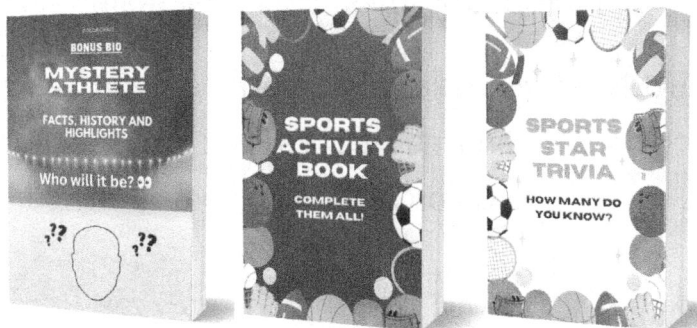

Just scan the QR code below or visit

bonus.colorcraftbooks.com/sports.

Scan to download. Kids: be sure to ask a parent first! ⬤

Thanks for reading.

Would you help us with a review?

If you enjoyed the book, we'd be so grateful if you could help us out by leaving a review on Amazon (even a super short one!). Reviews help us so much - in spreading the word, in helping others decide if the book is right for them, and as feedback for our team.

If you'd like to give us any suggestions, need help with something, or to find more books like this, please visit us at ColorCraftBooks.com.

Thank you

Thank you so much for picking up *All About Neymar Jr*. We really hope you enjoyed it and learned a lot about this extraordinary athlete.

Thanks again,

The Color Craft team

Made in United States
North Haven, CT
21 May 2025

69072703R00055